HITTING
ROCK BOTTOM

Defeating Depression, A Sure To Guide On How To Regain Control Over Your Life

**BY
CHRIS BROWN**

HITTING ROCK BOTTOM: *Defeating Depression, A Sure to Guide on How to Regain Control Over Your Life*

Copyright © 2020 by Chris Brown

All Right Reserved.

No part of this publication may be reproduced, distributed, or transmitted in any form or by any means, including photocopying, recording, or other electronic or mechanical methods, or by any information storage and retrieval system without the prior written permission of the publisher, except in the case of very brief quotations embodied in critical reviews and certain other noncommercial uses permitted by copyright law.

CONTENTS

INTRODUCTION 1
UNDERSTANDING MENTAL HEALTH DISORDERS 5
CHAPTER 1: *The Big Bully Depression* 7
CHAPTER 2: *Crushing Your Anxiety* 19
CHAPTER 3: *Magnitude Of Stress* 31
CHAPTER 4: *Don't Let Fear Control You* 37
CHAPTER 5: *When To Seek Treatment* 41
STRATEGIES FOR ALLEVIATING DEPRESSION, ANXIETY, STRESS, AND FEAR 45
CHAPTER 6: *All Natural Healing For Your Mind And Body* 47
CONCLUSION 59

INTRODUCTION

Merriam Webster's dictionary defines a stigma as a mark of shame or discredit. Mental illness has long carried a stigma, especially in certain cultures and communities. Among those groups, admitting you were depressed or dealing with anxiety was somehow a mark of shame. Moreover, getting help by going to a therapist or counselor was viewed as something only people from a different culture or community would do. Yet, if honest, most people would admit that they have been depressed, stressed out, anxious, or fearful at some point in their life. Temporarily experiencing these emotions does not necessarily mean you have a mental illness. The danger is when you experience these feelings frequently without treatment and when you experience them for a prolonged period of time.

Depression, anxiety, stress, and fear affect not only the individual but also the people closest to them. Several studies show that depressed parents negatively affect the positive experiences of their children. They are not able to participate actively in their child's upbringing, and low spirits caused by depression may make their children feel unloved or abandoned. This is something that me, and my sister tiffany experienced greatly with our mother Lisa Brown as she battled with her depression since the late 90's. While you would think most mothers would be into fashion, social gatherings, and working at a steady job for the rest of their lives.

Our mother was the complete opposite. Even though she did manage to maintain a position for 14 years with sprint telephone company, which now today is known as century link. Her depression became so unbearable that it ceased her from retiring from that position. My mother hasn't worked since 1994 and it is now the year 2020 that was 26 years ago!

Mental illness is sometimes a silent killer and has numerous effects. In some households, the yelling and tension that permeates their atmospheres is a direct result of unacknowledged mental illness experienced by parents who do not even think of getting help. It becomes part of a tainted family atmosphere that no one seems to acknowledge as unhealthy. That is what a stigma can do. *Frontiers in Public Health* has this to say about stigma.

> The stigma around depression and other mental illnesses can be higher in some cultural groups and

often is a major barrier to people from diverse cultures when accessing mental health services. Stigma can cause people to feel so ashamed that they hide their symptoms and do not seek treatment until the issues become major. Similarly, research with African American and Latino communities in the US also raises issues of mistrust of clinicians as a product of historical persecution as well as current issues of racism and discrimination. The challenges that this discussion on the historical perspective raises is around mental health systems that can work in more collaborative and power-sharing ways, and that work deliberately toward empowering the communities that they work within.

Frontiers in Public Health is suggesting what we know as an unspoken truth. Because of historical racism, some cultural groups are innately suspicious and mistrusting of clinicians and treatment in general. Why? To these cultures, clinicians and treatment represent the dominant, oppressive culture, so they disregard treatment altogether because they expect to be taken advantage of in the process.

Also, stigma is propagated in certain cultures because those who seek therapy are deemed as crazy or weak. Collectivistic cultures rely on one another. And it has been said that therapy is an individualistic practice that abandons the strength found in faith, community, and plain hard work to preserve through challenges. But, as indicated, the danger is that people in these communities try to hide or mask their symptoms until the problem is so severe that there is no way to continue to avoid it.

Yet another part of the stigma results from miseducation about what mental illness is; the general population lacks understanding about these illnesses. Besides, most do not utterly understand what depression, anxiety, stress, and fear are and how they impact not only mental health but also physical health as well. To gain more of an understanding, let's examine each of these negative emotions and discuss how they can affect an individual's life.

UNDERSTANDING MENTAL HEALTH DISORDERS

CHAPTER 1

THE BIG BULLY DEPRESSION

> *There will be tremendous storms in your life battling depression. But within you lies the resilience to make the sun shine again*

Depression is a big bully and mental health disorder characterized by persistently depressed mood or loss of interest in activities causing significant impairment in daily life. Of all mental illnesses, depression affects individuals at the highest rate. It has been known to keep you beat down, feeling sorry for yourself, out of mix, and dealing with life's difficulties in solitary confinement. Let's attempt to define depression and remove the stigma. As we dive deeper into what the illness really is, you will see that it can affect almost anyone at any time. First, we will distinguish sadness, from situational depression, and finally clinical depression.

Sadness

Everyone has experienced sadness. Now and then, something will happen, or a sad memory will surface that causes the feeling of sorrow to emerge. Someone who is experiencing sadness may cry or vent to a friend or family member. They may feel down, but the difference is the person can usually find relief and get past their sadness after expressing their emotions in one way or another. Sadness passes with time and does not impede daily functioning. A temporary sadness can be something as simple as, not having enough money in your bank account at that present moment. But still one must take into careful consideration having enough food to eat, a steady roof over your head, decent clothes to wear, and a reliable car to transport you back and forth from work. It's all in perspective. One can easily get caught up in the misfortunes of not having what they want at that current moment they desire it. But fail to realize what they already possess and should be thankful for in the process. If you are unhappy with the current amount of money that you are earning it may be time for an increase in skills and personal development so that you are able to live a more comfortable and satisfying life for you and your family. Remember, life is all about growth.

HITTING ROCK BOTTOM

Individuals will downplay the importance of working in their desired field and study, to stay at a job working a 9 to 5 that they absolutely hate. You must understand, this can cause you a great deal of sadness and pain to your emotional and overall well-being when you are not serving your true gifts, talents, and abilities. Always remember that you were created for a very special assignment on this planet called earth. If you feel you are having problems discovering your gifts, talents, and abilities send me an email at cthomasbrown89@gmail.com for a complimentary 1 on 1 30 minute coaching session to get you headed on the right track.

You also have to realize that if you are currently facing a sadness, everyday won't be sunshine and rainbows. Sorry if that sounds harsh but it's just the truth. There will be some days when you question who you are, and why in the world are you even here. But that's all part of the whole process of you being a human-being and discovering your existence so don't feel bad. Let me tell you a funny story. I remember days when I use to get so upset and bent out of shape over the craziest things. My birthday is on May 3, 1989, and for my 31st birthday my fiancé bought me Olive Garden followed by a dozen of Krispy Kreme Glazed Donuts YUM! When there were only 3 donuts left, I told her that I wanted the 2 and she could have the last one. But as soon as she was getting ready to open her mouth with a response, my stepson said

MA CAN I HAVE A DONUT! She looked me in the eyes and said yes baby. After I just told her I wanted the last 2 donuts she gave one of them to him. Can you believe that I was upset about that. Now you may be laughing so hard right now that your probably about to wet your pants, and I know this story probably doesn't possibly pertain to what you could be facing right now. But I thought I would just give you an example of how some of the things that make us sad or upset, can sometimes turn out to be the silliest of matters.

Now. Maybe that story I just shared with you has brought some kind of awareness to a particular person or event that had caused you a great deal of sadness and enforced you to get out of character. But now that the situation is behind you, here's a chance for you to sit back and reflect on how menial it may have been. Another way that we can experience sadness, is by not learning how to forgive others that have hurt us in the past. For example, let's just say a friend that you know said some pretty ugly things about you behind your back. And when word got back to you about this mishap, it left you emotionally scarred and completely puzzled. Then the next thing you know, you don't even want to be bothered with that so called friend ever again because your heart has been left completely torn by betrayal.

Afterwards, you go around carrying all that emotional baggage, sadness, and hatred with you for years because of this person. Even after that so called friend is long gone and living there best life in the future, and has completely forgotten about you. Your still sad, beat down, and in the dumps because you aren't able to progress from the past pain that the person has caused you. A small note to remember, we never really forgive a person for their sake. Even though it is the right and noble thing to do. We always forgive others so that we can have peace of mind, sanity, prosperity, and abundance in our own lives. Always remember that. Let's look at a quick fact from goodtherapy.org.

A research study from goodtherapy.org states that, Even though sadness is often linked with unfavorable circumstances, it is not always perceived in a negative light. Many people enjoy watching sad movies or listening to sad music because crying can be emotionally soothing. And while sadness can lead to withdrawal from other people or a loss of interest in certain activities, it can also prompt pleasure-seeking behaviors. In fact, positive personality traits such as alertness, thoughtfulness, and resilience can be fostered through sad experiences. Let's do a small exercise on what you just previously read about different examples of sadness. And the different ways that a sadness can be created. After you answer these simple questions, we will move on to our next form of depression Situational.

SMALL EXERCISE

List 3 examples of when someone or something caused you a great deal of sadness. What was you're responses to these events? If your response was negative what could you have done differently to produce a more positive result and outcome.

1.

2.

3.

Situational Depression

Situational depression lasts longer than sadness but not longer than clinical depression, and it is usually caused by a dramatic life change such as divorce, loss of job, a serious accident, or other major life changes such as retirement. Typically, situational depression lasts no longer than six months and affects men and women alike. Situational depression usually takes place within ninety days of an incident (triggering situation) and can usually be resolved as the individual takes steps to accept and adapt to the new situation. Another example of how situational depression might occur is the death of a loved one. As part of grief, the person may be in denial about their loss and may not be able to move past the situational depression until they accept the loss. Out of all, the situational depression examples that were just provided for you above divorce, job loss, accident, retirement, and death of a loved one. The loss of a loved one has greatly impacted my life the most. And it may be different for you.

My grandmother Mattie Foy played a major role in my life growing up as a child into adulthood. I can't think of anyone right now who would tell you that their grandmother didn't play a key role in their life. Especially when it came to cooking, because I absolutely love to eat her food, and throwing down in the kitchen was her specialty. Mattie Foy my grandmother and my grandfather Joseph Foy basically raised me, and my sister tiffany because my mother was in and out of the hospital due to her chronic depression. Mattie Foy the lady of my life, my rock passed away at the age of 96 in 2016. She lived a beautiful life full of love and contribution always giving back to the world and helping others. It was very hard for me to grasp the understanding of why she had to die. But like everything else on this planet, people are put here to serve a purpose, live their life, maximize to their full potential, and then return back to which they came from, there original home.

Maybe you're having a hard time dealing with a death in your family like I once was when my grandmother passed away. Trust me, the best thing that you can do in this situation is to find a close friend or family member that you can sit down with and express with deep emotion the way you are dealing with this painful loss. A lot of times we as human beings want to hold everything in that we are going through negatively in our lives. Not realizing that the emotional pain that we keep encamped inside of us, causes us to be worse off then we were before. Let's see what healthline.com has to say about situational depression.

Healthline.com says that however, supportive psychotherapy is generally the preferred treatment for situational depression as the treatment can help enhance coping mechanisms and resilience. This is important because it can help you cope with future challenges and potentially avoid future bouts of situational depression. One type of therapy that may help is cognitive behavioral therapy (CBT).

Now, I don't know what challenges you may be facing at this current moment. But situational depression like sadness is only temporary and is most definitely subject to change for the better. If you are interested in learning how to overcome challenges, struggles, and setbacks. I would strongly recommend that you read my ebook (Christopher Brown The Process Of Life) on Amazon.com. In this ebook I go into great detail and explain how we as human beings should not expect to live a problem free life. But having a positive mental attitude towards our difficulties will ultimately grant us the success that we desire. If you are interested in reading (The Process Of Life) here is the link www.amazon.com/dp/B07-RQ2KBDJ. Just to note, the copy of this book is (KINDLE UNLIMITED VERSION ONLY). Our last and final type of depression is Clinical.

Just to warn you before we move along, this is by far the worst type of depression that a person could possibly have or face in their life-time. And if any of these facts that you are about to read resonate with you on Clinical Depression, please seek out medical attention immediately.

Clinical Depression

Clinical depression is a long-lasting depression illness that prevents an individual from daily functioning. This type of depression can persist longer than six months. Symptoms may include:

- Thoughts of death or suicide
- Lack of focus and concentration
- Guilt
- Worthlessness
- Fatigue
- Change in sleep pattern
- Weight fluctuation
- Isolation
- Lack of interest in life
- A persisting depressed mood

Now, I'm going to be upfront and completely honest with you. I am a true believer of parents passing down genetics and traits to their children. I am also a firm believer that the type of environment that you are brought up in, and the people you are around the most has a tremendous affect on the way your life will eventually turn out. Earlier, in the introduction I gave you a very brief statement that my mother had, and still suffers to this day from depression.

In her case though, she has been diagnosed and considered to have clinical depression because of the amount of time the illness has persisted in her life. Which has been about 26 years. There would be some days when my mother wouldn't want to eat, sleep, talk, go outside, or be around anyone. That even sometimes included me, and my sister. You name the situation and that was the case. Now just from me naming those few simple things that a (normal) person would do on a regular daily basis, would probably make your stomach turn if you had a family member who didn't like to engage in these things. You would want to know what was wrong, how could you help, and is there possibly a cure for what you would think of as a small inconvenience.

The truth is, there is no cure for clinical depression. There are only things that can be done to alleviate the illness. Clinical depression is the most severe form of depression there is, and if it is not treated, may lead to death via suicide. So after experiencing my mother's depression majority of my life, it most definitely started to take its toll on me as you could imagine. Before I knew it I was taking antidepressants, going to go see a psychiatrist regularly, and getting admitted into crossroads, which is a psychiatric ward at the hospital all at the same time. When I was admitted into a psychiatric ward, it wasn't because I was losing my mind, or going crazy. You just have to understand that I was at a very low point in my life and was mentally damaged by the things that were going on around me.

There's something that I'm about to share with you during those dark days of my life that I have never told anyone before so brace yourself. When I was suffering from depression right before I got admitted into crossroads. I owned a 20 Gauge

Pump Action Shotgun. One day while I was sitting on the edge of my bed just thinking about my life and how unhappy I was. My shotgun came to mind while I was in deep thought. I went to my bedroom closet, opened the door, pulled out the gun, and sat back down on my bed. I then placed the shotgun in my mouth and sat there in complete silence.

I wanted to know the exact feeling of a victim who was about to commit suicide. Let me also clarify that the shotgun was unloaded. As I sat there and thought, and thought, and thought I pulled the shotgun out of my mouth and came to the realization that I am not that brave and bold of a soul to take my own life. But the very day that I did such of an act is the same day I got rid of that shotgun because I never wanted that to be the conclusion of my life nor for what I was remembered for.

I would just like to note as well, that it just wasn't me experiencing my mother's depression that led me to my illness. It was a series of events that drove me to that point. Just to list a few were 1. Not wanting to see my grandmother pass away 2. I was unclear about what my purpose was in life 3. Not being able to keep a steady and reliable job just to name a few. If you are every feeling like I once was, considering testing out the theory of what it would be like to take your own life. Let me just tell you that it's not worth it, you have a lot to live for and contribute back to this world. As well as family members, and friends who would miss you dearly if you decided to do so.

Please Contact National Suicide Prevention at (1-800-273-8255) if you are ever thinking of causing bodily harm to yourself. Help is always available to you.

HITTING ROCK BOTTOM

I am happy to say though me, and my mother are doing extremely better now as time has progressed. Even though she still battles from depression and takes medication for it daily. It is nowhere near as bad as it once was when she was at that low point in her life.

But hey, that's enough about me it's time to create some positive change in your own life!

Positive Affirmations for Your Life

This is just a little something that I thought I would share with you to help reconstruct some of the outer and inner negative conversations that you may be having with yourself. I've noticed that the mind for some strange reason loves to replay and recite the negative past experiences that we've been through. Thoughts and feelings of not being good enough, feelings of being stupid, feeling fat, feeling ugly, not being tall enough, not short enough, not feeling smart enough etc. That is exactly why I created these positive affirmations that I would love for you to repeat to yourself out loud in your private setting if you wish. These positive sayings are just reinforcing and bringing back to life what's already inside of you. Please repeat these affirmations to yourself first when you arise in the morning, and right before you turn in for bed at night. Are you ready? Here we go. Say

1. I AM BOLD
2. I AM BRIGHT
3. I AM BEAUTIFUL
4. I AM CREATIVE
5. I AM CAPABLE
6. I AM GOOD LOOKING
7. I AM INTELLIGENT

8. I AM HAPPY
9. I AM OPTIMISTIC
10. I AM POSITIVE
11. I AM WEALTHY
12. I AM PROSPEROUS
13. I AM SUCCESFUL
14. I AM HEALTHY
15. GREAT THINGS ARE COMING MY WAY

You may be feeling like a brand-new person already, eager and ecited to tackle the world by just repeating those simple affirmations look at you go! Now just saying those positive affirmations is one thing in itself. But saying them and believing them is a completely different matter, you must believe. Time for our Depression Check!

DEPRESSION CHECK

Are you experiencing any of the symptoms of situational or clinical depression? Be honest and reflect on your lifestyle, interactions, sleep patterns, etc. Are there any patterns that have persisted more than a few months? Have you experienced any trauma(s) that may have impacted your mood? If so list them.

CHAPTER 2

CRUSHING YOUR ANXIETY

Having rushing or negative thoughts can be due to the anticipation of something bad happening around you, or to you. The main goal is to not let those events control your mind.

To experience occasional anxiety does not constitute a mental illness. However, professionals categorize frequent feelings of intense or excessive anxiety that impair daily functioning as anxiety disorder. The feelings of anxiety can also be the result of stressors or trauma such as a war injury, car crash, large crowds, sexual assault, paying bills, or similar events. Such feelings if pro-longed, can also be categorized as an anxiety disorder. Part of the disorder is that the magnitude and frequency of the anxiety typically exceed the impact of the event. Examples of what health care professionals call anxiety disorders include panic attacks, post-traumatic stress disorder (PTSD), and obsessive-compulsive disorder etc. Now that we've just read a more factual definition of anxiety disorder, let's break it down to were it's even more understandable. Here's our first example. (**Paying Bills)**

When I was growing up as a child into my teenage years, I never really experienced anxiety before. It wasn't until I became an adult when the attacks of anxiety started to make their grand entrance into my life. My problem was always trying to properly managing my income. And the reason I say that is because I always had a tendency of spending every cent I made once I got paid from either my job or if money was given to me generously by another person. And then when it was time for me to pay the bills I was extremely short on cash. But as a child and teenager, it's very rare that you have any big or major responsibilities to fulfill at all growing up. And that's because we will more than likely have tremendous support and help from our parents and loved ones.

But sooner or later, once you move on from the nest of your parents comfort adult reality will set in. One can expect to be paying light bill, water bill, car payment, gas, groceries, on top of supporting children if you have any at that particular time in your life. With all these responsibilities you could imagine how anxiety could easily creep into your everyday living. Especially if you're working at a job that isn't paying you enough money to support your needs. Fortunately enough for me though once I met my now fiancé soon to be wife, we decided to sit down together and strategically map out our bills 1 by 1 and now have a great understanding of what needs to be paid around the house so that it's not to much of a strain for either of us. But maybe it's still a little tight for you even if you do have a strategic plan in place. If you and your spouse are living together and are having to much month left at the end of your money. Then maybe one of you should think about taking up some additional work or, releasing some of your household items that have lesser value and could be sold for money to get you ahead on your bills.

If you are single then maybe you should consider downsizing to something smaller than what you are currently living in right now. A lot of individuals like to do what I call (trying to keep up with the joneses). Living in or renting something that looks extravagant to the outside world, but in reality is killing your pockets dearly. This will cause you a deal great of anxiety, because it will be hard for you to get ahead mentally and financially for your future. Whatever the case may be. Know that anxiety is something that we will all experience from time to time no matter what the cost or situation is. Some anxiety is easily avoidable, and in other situations and circumstances it may not be. Let's look at our second example. (**Car Crash**)

A few personal stories that I can share with you that not only happened to me once but twice was, getting into 2 major car crashes. Now, I don't know if any of you have ever been in a car accident before, but let me be the first one to tell you. (1). It's scary as all hell! And (2). I thought I was going to die. It was only by the graces of God that I made it out alive, and luckily neither accidents were my fault. But both cars were deemed as total losses when it was all said and done. The first accident that happened was when I was with my cousin Terrell. I was riding in the passenger seat of his Chevy SS and we were coming back from the store after picking up a few items, and a lady slowly pulls out right in front of us when her stop light was red. I was looking at Terrell talking to him about something. Now what it was, I can't remember. Then the next thing I know he's slamming on brakes. I refocus my attention to the front of his car and I'm presented with a vehicle right in front of my face! (BAM)!!! Anxiety wasn't the word for me. I could literally see my heart beating through my chest before we hit that car. After we struck the vehicle. The only thing that I could do was cough profusely due to all the smoke that had risen from the airbags being deployed. I immediately got out of the car limping, and walked as far as I could away from the crash site not being sure if it was going to explode with us still inside of it due to the impact. I then fell to the ground and laid on my back face covered in tears looking up at the pitch black sky still shaking in shock. And the only thing that could come out of my mouth was (THANK YOU JESUS). I probably said that 100 times while I was laying there until the ambulance came. It was a blessing me, and my cousin escaped out of that accident that night with only minor injuries and bruises after being transported to the hospital.

    The second time, I was by myself driving my grandmother's Pontiac G6. And the same thing happened only this time it was a man not a women. He also ran a red light, and I ran smack dab right into the side of him. Also known as a T- bone accident. A T- bone accident is were someone fails to yield to the driver that has the right of way. Usually, one driver will accidentally make a dangerous left turn at an intersection, thinking the other car will stop at a yellow traffic light. I was so upset and mad about that second car accident that I was in, because my grandmother had basically given me that car and it was paid for. Plus I had all the minor repairs done to it so I was riding in style. The next thing I know, it gets totaled just like that.

But there is something valuable that I did gain from both of those 2 accidents. And that's my life. You can always get another car Chris my cousin Lisa Mcdaniel once told told me, but you can never get another life. Plus, it prompted me to get the car of my dreams. My dream car is not A Lamborghini, Mercedes AMG, BMW, or a Ferrari. It's a plain Dodge Challenger with the Hemi in it. It's just something about the body style of that car that screams muscle and manliness! So if you look at it in a bigger perspective it was most definitely a win for me.

Let's continue on with our examples dealing with. (**Large Crowds**).

Large crowds of people may also cause the feelings of anxiety as well. Naturally I am an extrovert. It's very easy for me to go up to complete strangers and start a full blown conversation with them because I absolutely love people. But at the same time, I can be an introvert were I can easily keep to myself and don't really care so much for being bothered because sometimes being around a lot of people makes me feel claustrophobic like I can't breathe. I guess you can call it a catch 22 thing for me in a nutshell. A research study from health.clevelandclinic.org says that, It may help to know that feelings of anxiety are normal. When being around large crowds many people may feel this uneasiness to some degree in the same situation.

If you're among those who find themselves feeling a bit claustrophobic when out and about, it's usually best to try and stay calm, says clinical psychologist Scott Bea, PsyD." If you feel your anxiety coming on, you might just want to try hanging in there, because we actually will recover from our anxiety or panic attack if you just stay put and don't try to fix what you're feeling," Dr. Bea says.

Dr. Bea also recommends standing or sitting still, and to keep your eyes up and looking out. Focus on maintaining natural breathing. Describe to yourself or your companion any uneasy feelings you're experiencing, then rate your level of discomfort.

Acknowledge to yourself that being around that large crowd is a choice, and you can leave at any moment. The panicky, anxious feelings should pass fairly soon, he says.

According to the Mayo Clinic, the causes of anxiety disorders are not fully understood. However, medical professionals have observed that some anxiety disorders can be linked to or caused by medical issues. For example, heart disease or a heart attack could be linked to anxiety as well as diabetes, hyperthyroidism, respiratory issues, chronic pain, and more.

Like depression, anxiety can cause a lack of focus and make it hard to concentrate. However, other symptoms deviate from those of depression. Other anxiety symptoms may include:

- Nervousness
- An expectation of danger and doom
- An accelerated heart rate
- Rapid breathing

- Weakness
- Tiredness
- Insomnia
- Gastrointestinal complications
- Uncontrolled worry
- Avoidance of things that might trigger anxiety

That's quite a list of symptoms when taken into careful consideration each individual effect that it has on your body. Currently while this book has been written, I work for a company called Moen Incorporated. Moen is a product line of faucets and other fixtures started by inventor Alfred M. Moen that is now part on the Fortune Brands Home & Security Company. The Moen subsidiary is headquartered in North Olmsted, Ohio. Moen was originally part of Ravenna Metal Products of Seattle, Washington. The facility building that I work at in New Bern North Carolina holds about 500-600 people split between a 1st and 2nd shift of workers. That's a lot of people split between 2 shifts in one building!

Before we go to our stations to begin our daily task. We do what I would like to call, light stretches and muscle tension alleviation. This is were we preform a series of different stretches and exercises to make sure that our body has been loosened up for the vigorous work assignment ahead of us. Normally, we all stand around in large groups of circles and begin our stretches lead by our Team Leader. I say all of that to say this to you. Sometimes when we are in our large group settings, my anxiety gets so bad from standing around so many people to the point were I have to literally go to the bathroom, sit in a stall, catch my breath, and regain my consciousness of the matter at hand. I know that may sound a little absurd to you but it's the truth. Anxiety is most definitely real. And if not taken care of properly, it will eventually weigh you down in the long run. You should never feel ashamed of having anxiety. My definition of the illness is, holding in to many problems, circumstances, and setbacks and not venting them clearly to a loved one or someone who cares to listen to what's going on in your life. There's always someone out there who is willing to have an open ear to what is going on in your journey. But you must open your mouth so you can be heard.

(War Injury) When I was trying to find out what my purpose was in life. I attempted to join the US Military some years ago after graduating from high school. But failed to do so, because I was unable to pass the ASVAB requirement test to enlist. Looking back on those days now, I can truly understand why I couldn't pass that test. It was because God had different plans for my life. And who knows the dangers I could have possibly been faced with out there on the frontlines. I've known a lot of men and women who have served for our country traveling all across the world on active duty. Some of those individuals retired from the service with over 20+ years in the military. And some with only 4 years of active duty in the service who were ready to get out. In my honest opinion, the difference between the individuals who serve 20+ years in the military vs. the ones who may have only served 4 years could be a combination of multiple contributing factors. 1. Expiration of enlistment, 2. Medical discharge/Disability, 3. Dependency and hardship, 4. Lack of fulfillment, 5. And last, other career plans and ideas. For me though, none of these were the case because I couldn't even enlist how funny is that. But there is an old friend of mine who did enlist and received a purple heart for his active duty service in the Marine Corps. The article that was written on him is by Heather King. And was posted Tuesday at 8:19am, January 4, 2011 on WITN.com.

And so it reads, a marine from New Bern North Carolina has been awarded the Purple Heart Medal in Afghanistan after he was hit by an IED. Cpl. Bryan Brown is a 20-year-old Marine who is based at Camp Pendleton in California but is currently deployed to Afghanistan. The Marine Corps released information stating Brown was hit by an IED on September 5. Cpl. Brown is a heavy equipment operator for the Marine Corps, a role which he describes driving large vehicles, such as tractors. He also helps build patrol bases in Helmand province. Cpl. Brown was part of the New Bern Bears High School Football Team that won the state championship in 2007 against Charlotte Independence Patriots.

Cpl. Brown is carrying on his family tradition of military service. He says his mother was in the Army, his father was in the Marine Corps, and his grandfather was in the Navy. Bryan suffered from a grade-three concussion from the explosion. In his words he said, "I received an award that previous Marines have received," said Brown, heavy equipment operator, Charlie Company. "It's an honor and emotional moment for me." Now I'm not positive if Bryan was medically discharged from the military after that incident took place or not. But I do know that was an experience for him like none other that has greatly affected his life in a major way.

And even though it's been a while since I've seen or talked to Bryan. I know all is well with him from our last conversation we had some years ago. We are also friends on Facebook and Instagram as a way of staying connected and following each other. But what courage he displayed in that critical moment in his life when he was hit by that IED in Afghanistan and received that purple heart. Let's continue on and have a look at our last and final possible cause of anxiety Sexual Assault.

(Sexual Assault) The term sexual assault refers to sexual contact or behavior that occurs without explicit consent of the victim. Some forms of sexual assault include: Attempted rape. Fondling or unwanted sexual touching. Forcing a victim to preform sexual acts, such as oral sex or penetrating the perpetrator's body.

I know for some of you that may have been a very explicit or even touchy definition of sexual assault. And by any means necessary if that definition has rubbed you the wrong way, or has triggered a negative emotion inside of you, I greatly do apologize. But sexual assault at it's core is just what the definition explains it to be. Words probably wouldn't even be able to express how vivid and painful of a memory that must have been for an individual who has ever been faced with such an unpleasant and unbearable circumstance.

I would also like to state that sexual assault isn't always about offenders getting pleasure from sex. It can also be about them enjoying asserting power and control over someone. Some offenders have been abused themselves, but this isn't always the case. Sexual assault is a serious crime and is never the fault of the survivor.

Going back to me talking about how sexual assault isn't just in the form of sexual acts. But could be in asserting power and control over someone, was the one that was greatly influenced on me the most. Peer Pressure, one acting Controlling towards another, and being Bullied are at an all time high in today's society. Not just as kids, but adults as well still deal with peer pressure, being controlled, and bullied to this day. Reflecting back on my life, I could just think of the times were someone would assert their power and dominion over me to do something wrong unconsciously on there behalf, and not even realize what they were doing at that present moment. And me lacking the level of awareness that I should have had was gullible enough to participate in such horrendous acts.

I remember the time when an old (who I thought to be was a friend), encouraged me to punch another guy in the face at a night party. Deon said Chris, you see Dee standing over there... I said yea, he said I want you to go over there and hit him straight in the face! And what did I do. I went over there, not even knowing the situation at hand of why he wanted me to punch him in the face and proceeded to do so anyway. When I walked up to Dee I stopped. Looked him square in the eyes, and held my fist clenched up as if I were a professional prize fighter about to go head to head with my oppressor. My heart was racing with confusion and anticipation of what was about to happen. As soon as I was about to make my move, I thought to myself what in the world am I doing? I'm about to punch this boy in the face because Deon told me to. Dee hasn't done anything to me. I kind of felt like he knew something was about to happen because he just stood there in silence. As I regained consciousness of who I was as an individual, I slowly backed off of him and went back to where Deon was standing. He said, WHY DIDN'T YOU PUNCH HIM IN THE FACE!!! I told Deon because you don't control me... A very powerful story. But just imagine how that may have turned out if I did proceed with what he had told me to do. It wouldn't have been pretty. That's just one of the many powers of people having the ability to control your actions so be careful.

In the next chapter were going to look at stress, and what are some of the main causes of this emotional and physical tension. So buckle up your seat belt and prepare for the ride!

ANXIETY CHECK

Are you experiencing any of the symptoms of an anxiety disorder? Are you potentially facing any medical conditions that might be connected to anxiety? If so, please consult with your healthcare official about what issues you may be having. A persons illness will only get worse with time the longer it is being delayed and put off.

CHAPTER 3

MAGNITUDE OF STRESS

> *When I look back on all these worries, I remember the story of the old man who said on his deathbed that he had a lot of trouble in his life, most of which that had never happened.*

One of the distinguishing features of stress is that it is physiological. Meaning, you often first feel its effects in your body. Stress is your body and brain's response to a situation or challenge, and it is not always bad. Your heart rate may accelerate, your breathing may become more pronounced, your muscles may become tenser, or you may begin to sweat.

Stress can sometimes signal you to safety. It can make you aware of a danger and take the necessary actions to change your environment and stay safe.

It's truly amazing though, how certain events can actually happen in our own lives that can cause us a great deal of stress. But it's even more amazing the invisible stressors that we can bring upon ourselves in our own physical mind before it even really happens. Let me ask you a question? How many times have you ever created a particular scenario or circumstance in your head and it never came to fruition? Probably a million times, and that seems to be the normal for most people. It really intrigues me though how the mind can produce hundreds if not thousands of negative thoughts each and everyday, but when we attempt to switch our thinking to a positive frame and standpoint to relieve the stress, the mind repels it. I wonder why? Let's dive a little bit deeper into stress related terms to try and find out what the reasoning may be.

Everyone experiences short-term stress because life is full of challenges. For example, students may experience stress in preparation for an exam. Parents may experience stress in preparation for sending a child off to college. People can experience stress when they have to meet a deadline or make a presentation for work. However, these stressors subside after the challenge is over, and your brain and body reset to a normal state. If your heart rate was accelerated, it slows back down to normal. Nervousness, sweat, and rapid breathing cease.

But when stress becomes long-term, it is terrible both physically and mentally because your body never gets a cue to reset. Coupled with that is the reality that some people deal with stress better than others. Some people are wired not to take things so seriously, while others overthink things by nature. With long-term stress, your brain and body remain in a stressed state, which creates wear and tear that leads to mental and physical breakdowns. Short-term stress can cause headaches, irritability, insomnia, anger, agitation, or sadness. But long-term stress can cause and accelerate major illnesses including, depression, anxiety, high blood pressure, diabetes, and more.

A doctor will typically diagnose stress by asking an individual about their symptoms and life events. Diagnosing stress can be challenging because it depends on many factors. Doctors have used questionnaires, biochemical measures, and physiological techniques to identify stress. However, these may not be objective or effective. The most direct way to diagnose stress and it's effects on a person is through a comprehensive, stress-oriented, face-to-face interview. If you remember earlier in Chapter 1., I gave you a list of events that caused me to develop a temporary state of depression. To refresh your memory, some of those events were. 1. Not wanting to see my Grandmother die because she meant the world to me 2. I was unclear about what my purpose was in life, and what I wanted to do 3. Last, me not being able to keep a steady and reliable job. I would also like to say that before everything I was going through negatively which caused my depression. They all started out as great stressors first and foremost.

We all have to realize that, whatever persistently stays on our mind and we focus on becomes our reality. Whether they are good things that are on our minds or bad things it doesn't really matter. Dwell on stressing factors long enough and they will most definitely come true for you. And so for me it was those 3 factors. Instead of me getting stressed out about my Grandmother dying, I could have looked at it in a different light. And realized that this is a temporary home for all of us and certainly everyone will die one day. Instead of me getting bent out of shape about what my purpose was in life, and what I wanted to do. That could have been time for me to really sit down plan, plot, and strategize on the things that I really wanted to accomplish in life. And instead of me being focused on why I couldn't keep a steady job. That should have been a clear indication for me that God had bigger and better plans for my life. But all those things that I was so focused on in particular caused me so much grief and stress. Now, that I am much older and wiser. I can look back on those days were I was stressed out and see how much I have grown spiritually, physically, mentally, and emotionally. Question? Is there something that you're dealing with in your life right now that is causing you tremendous stress and heartache?

If there is, please take into careful consideration what those stressors are. Because 9/10 most of the things that we put big and major emphasis on in our lives are really minor issues that could be solved very efficiently and quickly. Let me share a little story with you. My sister Tiffany who now resides in the state of Columbia South Carolina never really knew how things were going to pan out for her making such a big and important move from North Carolina to South Carolina. Everything she needed to make the transition was already lined up for her to make the initial move. She had the car, she saved up the money, and she had the new highly paid job offer. Outside looking in, all of ducks were lined up straight in a row. The only problem was, she was having a very difficult time finding a place to stay because her credit score was a little low. I mean let's be completely honest here. Who hasn't faced some kind of trail and error with trying to build and replenish there credit score. We all do or did at some point in time. My sister was so stressed out and nervous about not being able to find a place to stay that, her faith started to slowly slip away. She looked to me, and my mother and said, what in the world am I going to do? No one will accept me because of my poor credit score. I looked my sister dead in the eyes and told her that, you cannot lose your faith Tiffany! I said trust me. If it's meant for you to be in Columbia South Carolina then God will most definitely make sure that it is fulfilled. And what do you know. She re-strengthen her faith, got approved for a beautiful spacious apartment on the top floor, and is doing very well for herself I must say. But you see, she put so much stress and fear in her heart of not finding a place to stay that her faith started to waver. But once she realized the negative emotions that she was experiencing of not getting the apartment. She had no other plan but to let every negative emotion that she was facing go. And to her dismay, everything that she had hoped and wished for fell right into place as it should have. So trust me, the thing that you are stressing over right now, LET IT GO! Because victory is surely on it's way. Time for our Stress Check!

STRESS CHECK

Are you in a long-term stress pattern? Do you have personal strategies for dealing with stress? Are there any unnecessary stressors in your life? Meaning, are there things that can be eliminated from your life that are causing stress? If so, take out a blank sheet of paper and pen and list your unnecessary stressors on your paper. Once you list all your unnecessary stressors, you will soon realize how small and menial they really are.

CHAPTER 4 DON'T LET FEAR CONTROL YOU

> *False Evidence Appearing Real is the only thing fear really stands for. Once I realized that, he was kindly asked to leave.*

In the context of mental health, fear is associated with phobias. A phobia is a fear of something or a particular situation. For example, agoraphobia is the fear of being alone in public places from which there is no easy escape. Mental health professionals classify phobias as specific or simple phobias, social phobias, and agoraphobia.

Specific or simple phobias are a fear of a particular situation or thing that in fact, may be safe. But when faced with being in the situation or around the thing, a phobia can bring a quick rush of panic. Specific phobias are varied and tailored to that particular person, and it is common for them to start in adolescence or adulthood. For example, someone traumatized by a dog attack in adolescence may have a fear of dogs into their adulthood. Someone that has gotten into a car crash in their adulthood years may have a fear of driving or even getting back on the open road. These phobias may or may not disappear over time.

Social phobias create a fear of being embarrassed or humiliated by people. It may also be a fear of being the center of attention, being judged by others, or being offended by others. Such phobias cause individuals to avoid people, groups, and social gatherings. The root of this phobia may be rejection or low self-esteem.

All through my life, I was joked and criticized about my educational background and being over weight. I some what felt inferior to the other students in the classroom because I couldn't seem to grasp the concept of what the teacher was trying to teach us. I was always the student in the classroom who was labeled to have a learning disability, had to receive extra time on my test so I could understand and complete it, and was separated from the other students and put in the front row section of the class because the other kids were a distraction to me. You can only imagine the negative mental and emotional effects that had on my self-esteem and confidence. And as a result of all that, I started to pick up weight tremendously my junior year in high school. Weighing in at a whopping 311 pounds! Now to me that's just outrageous and uncalled for weighing that much only to be a junior in high school. But I had such a low self-esteem and lack of confidence in myself, that food was my only alternative and outlet that gave my pure joy. My only single outlet was eating emotionally obsessively.

So whenever I was approached to engage in open conversation with my teacher and fellow classmates. I would have some sort of fear in my heart because I felt a conversation would be spawned up either pertaining to how I was doing in class or the amount of weight that I was carrying around. So engaging in open conversation back then, even until this day is still slightly a negative phobia for me. Because, the mental trauma that I was carrying around for so long. If you are just now hearing this from someone let me be the first one to say that having a negative mental phobia is perfectly fine. As long as you know that any negative mental phobia that you are facing is very well surmountable and. With persistent effort, and applied application of learning how to get over the phobia you are facing, success lies right around the corner from you!

I know your probably saying to yourself, who does he think he is. Telling me that I can get over this phobia that I've been facing for years. He has no idea what I'm going through. Let me just tell you that if a man can overcome the odds of being joked about his weight and criticized about his educational standings all throughout his life, had to repeat the 4th and the 10th grade twice, and didn't graduate out of high school until he was 20 years old. Then you to my good friend have the ability to overcome any phobia, fear, setback, or challenge that you are going through. But it requires a strong belief in yourself, and a strong belief that you are capable of getting over your phobia and back in control of your life. I STRONGLY BELIEVE IN YOU, BUT YOU ALSO MUST HAVE GREAT BELIEF IN YOURSELF. Time for our Phobia Check!

PHOBIA CHECK

Are there any situations or things that has caused phobias in your life? Were there any events in your adolescence or adulthood years that has caused you to fear certain situations? This is a time right now for you to be completely honestly and upfront with yourself. Are you afraid of being embarrassed around people or get nervous when you are around social gatherings? If so, please list your different types of emotions and feelings. After you have written them down. Think of certain ways that could help you alleviate some of those phobias and fears.

CHAPTER 5

WHEN TO SEEK TREATMENT

> A persistent negative feeling in the mind and in your emotions may be due to underlying mental health issues that require serious medical attention.

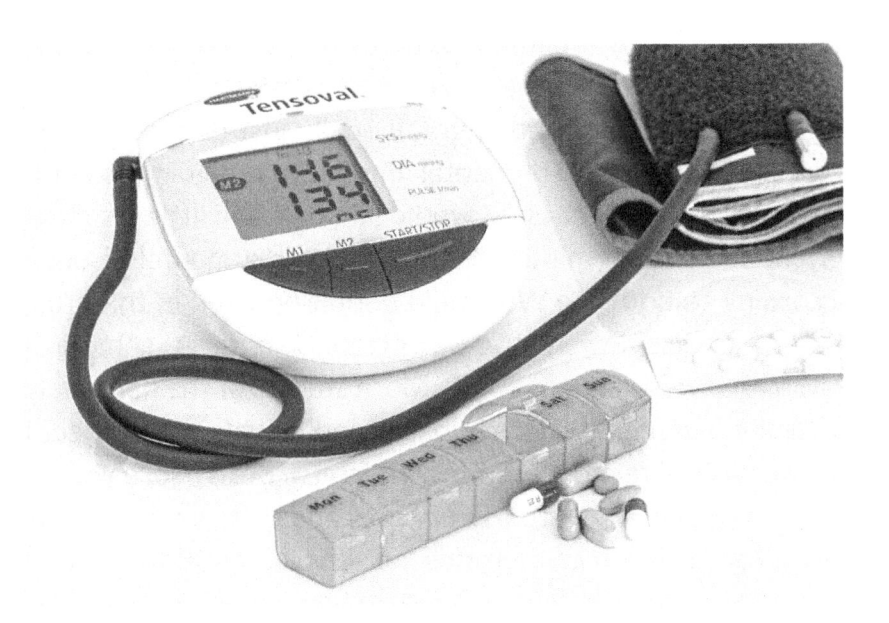

This is probably the most important Chapter in this book, out of all the other 5 Chapters. Clinical depression impairs daily functioning. However, if you are feeling depressed, you do not have to wait until your ordinary everyday functioning is impaired to seek medical treatment. If your relationships at home are in danger due to your illness, or your level of focus at work is at an all time low, talk to a mental health professional or counselor as soon as possible. Speaking to someone early on can prevent progression into an acute or dangerous situation and protect the most important relationships in your life.

    As noted earlier, depression can have a huge negative effect on your mental and physical life. One could even take into consideration committing suicide, or even worse. Taking the life of someone else. Example. One individual may get so depressed and ill that they may just want to stay locked up in their room all day and night and not be bothered by anyone. Another individual may get depressed and become outrageously violent and angry. It really just depends on the person and their level of mental illness. I'm not going to get to deep into this subject. But I would like to talk a little bit about Psychopaths for a minute. Psychopathy is a mental disorder according to both the Wakefield definition cited in this study and American Psychiatric Association criteria (American Psychiatric Association, 2000). More studies of the harm done to family members by psychopathic individuals are needed. If you are still alive and breathing, which I'm pretty sure you are if you're reading this book. Every now and then you have come across or heard tragic stories of school shootings, church massacres, and cop killings. I mean, how could you have not heard about them. That's all our Newspapers and News Channels pump into our lives any way. The Columbine shooting on April 20, 1999 at Columbine High School in Littleton, Colorado, occurred when two teens went on a shooting spree, killing 13 people and wounding more than 20 others, before turning their guns on themselves and committing suicide. Or what about the Charleston church shooting (also known as the Charleston church massacre) was a mass shooting on June17, 2015, in Charleston, South Carolina, in which nine African Americans were killed during a Bible study at the Emanuel African Methodist Episcopal Church.

And finally, the death of Mr. George Floyd. The man who was apprehended by the Minneapolis Minnesota police department, on May 25, 2020 and was killed. The main suspect of the murder Derek Chauvin would become known around the entire world for putting his knee on the neck of George Floyd during an arrest and holding it there for more than eight minutes, until Mr. George no longer had a pulse. I know your probably thinking to yourself. Chris, what do all these tragedies have to do with depression? Well, I'm glad you asked. If you look very closely, each individual who was involved in a serious murder, had some sort of mental health issue or is still facing that illness today. I mean really, you just don't wake up one day, take a shower, eat your breakfast, kiss your family goodbye before you leave the house, and then go viciously and brutally kill someone! And if you did, those are underlying mental health issues that someone should have spotted in that person while they were still in adolescence. Maybe it could have been a much different outcome for those brave people who lost their lives to senseless carnage. I know that may have gotten a little off track from knowing when to seek treatment. But I feel that it was very important and necessary to talk about. And how psychopathy can be related to depression as well. Let's get back into what we were discussing earlier about the stigma.

Remember that the stigma is unmerited. Everyone feels depressed, anxious, stressed, or afraid at some point in there life. Talking to someone can ensure your feelings do not progress into a serious clinical disorder. I REPEAT (DO NOT WAIT) UNTIL A PERFECT TIME TO SEEK MEDICAL ATTENTION IF YOU ARE NOT FEELING WELL.

Also, be sure you take advantage and invest in strategies that cost nothing at all to you, to alleviate the signs of mental illnesses and depression. This is a personal theory of mine. When visiting a doctor for a particular matter or reason. The first ideal thing for them to do is to prescribe some sort of medication to the patient who is facing the effects of an illness, health condition, or health disorder. The doctors will always tell you how the drug you are about to consume is going to help you win in the area that you are struggling in. But never note to mention the tremendous negative side effects the drug may pose on your brain and body as well. I'm not trying to take anything away from the doctor's who have been put here on earth to serve us in a major way and bring us back to regular functioning health. But in my honest opinion, I do not feel like every sickness or illness has to be resulted to and remedied by a prescription drug. There are also other natural cures, strategies, and remedies that one can pursue that may have the same positive effect on your body or greater done right at your home in your wonderful leisure time.

STRATEGIES FOR ALLEVIATING DEPRESSION, ANXIETY, STRESS, AND FEAR

Now that we have explained each of these areas, it is essential to explore ways to deal with and alleviate depression, anxiety, stress, and fear. In Chapter 6: All Natural Healing For Your Mind And Body. I will share with you a few secrets on how you can use all natural cures to your benefit.

CHAPTER 6

ALL NATURAL HEALING FOR YOUR MIND AND BODY

> *There's always a second enlightening alternative to a problem you're facing. Sometimes it just requires a second opinion from a different source.*

I really hope you have enjoyed this book, as we finally get ready to come to a close with All Natural Healing For Your Mind And Body. Please note, that I am in no way a psychiatrist, mental health worker, doctor, or physician. That if you feel you are in the need of serious medical attention, please seek help! Chapter 6 is based on my experience battling depression and the steps I took to alleviate the illness. So with that being said, please let's continue. When I was taking antidepressants and seeing my psychiatrist twice a month. I started to realize that the treatment that I was receiving from both sources my psychiatrist and the antidepressant pills were not helping my problems and depression at all in my most honest opinion. It wasn't until I started doing these activities below, and shifting my mindset from a negative frame to positive standpoint that I started to see major changes in my life. And hopefully major change will present itself to you in a positive way as well. Let's begin shall we.

Exercise

First and foremost, if you are at risk for depression or stress disorders, or currently feeling depressed or stressed, make sure getting exercise is a top priority for you. This is something that has always worked wonders for me. I always make sure that I'm pushing myself to my greatest limit when I'm working out. As I am writing this book, we are now in what I would call a pandemic due to covid-19. The Coronavirus has most definitely changed the world of everyday living and normal activities for every individual on the planet. It has even gotten to the point were public gyms are closed and are no longer in operation due to social distancing. And a lot of us know how filthy and nasty some of our gyms can be nowadays. So to a certain degree, I don't blame gym owners for shutting down their facilities to keep people safe and out of harms way. But with majority of all gym closings, that leaves a lot of people in the dark about how they can proceed with their regular workout regimen.

HITTING ROCK BOTTOM

Now, I can't speak for anyone else on how they are continuing to get their exercise in. But one of the things that I like to do is, go back to my old high school and workout at the football field and track. Normally how I like to start my workout off is by doing a light full body stretch. Followed by a 1 to 2 mile job, just to get the blood flowing. I incorporate pushups, sit-ups, squats, jump rope, tire flips, and pull-ups on the football field goal to make sure that I am getting a full body workout. The only downside to exercising outside is that it's outside. So with that being said, you are always open to different climate changes and conditions. But to me in my honest opinion, exercising outside has a tremendous benefit for you because the air is more dense and thicker. Versus you working out in the gym where they have AC and it's a little bit easier to breathe. I know that may sound crazy to you. And working out in a gym is more comfortable and convenient. But I do believe you should always be doing things that are challenging you, and pushing you to the next level of your greatest true self. Here's an exercise fact!

According to WebMD, exercise gives you a positive boost in mood and leads to lower rates of depression. Why? Well, one reason is that when you exercise, your body releases a chemical called endorphins, and endorphins act like sedatives and create euphoria. Regular exercise has been proven to reduce stress, improve the quality of sleep, and alleviate feelings of anxiety and depression.[1] Also, an added benefit of exercise is that if done consistently, your resulting new and improved body may boost your self-esteem and confidence. Low self-esteem is connected to some phobias and

---

.

depression. Thus, exercise can help in diverse and positive ways.

And just about any type of exercise can help with depression. You do not have to be an athlete or bodybuilder. Taking a walk in the sun get's you moving and has the added benefit of getting you Vitamin D, which can better your mood. Dancing, yard work, and house cleaning all qualify as exercises that can help alleviate a depressed mood. A group exercise class may also provide emotional connection and support as well as physical benefits.

Amend Your Schedule For Small Successes

If you are stressed or depressed, you may feel as if you have lost control of your days. Also, your everyday routine may seem overwhelming. If that is the case, focus on small achievable tasks and plan your day accordingly. To start, you may not be able to do everything you would typically do in a day. Start small and work your way up. A little something I like to do to amend my schedule is called the (Law Of Priority). The night before I go to bed. I examine and analyze the most important things that need attention for the next day. Remember, the mind always has a way of making it seem like you have 101 things to do. Constantly racing all over the place to get nowhere. But if you plan your day out in advance, the night before you go to bed with a blank sheet of paper and pen in hand. It will really narrow down the amount of things one has to accomplish for maximum productivity.

Be sure to celebrate your small achievements to boost your sense of accomplishment and foster motivation to do the next small task or step. For example, sometimes bills can pile up when you experience depression. It feels too overwhelming to tackle them all. So, start with paying one bill a day or negotiating with one bill collector a day if that is the case for you. Eventually, after working your way through these smaller tasks, the number will reduce, and it will not feel so overwhelming to you. Steady and persistence always wins the race.

Relax

Because depression, stress, anxiety, and fear can all affect your sleep patterns, finding ways to relax and unwind may better your mood and allow you to proceed with your regular sleeping. Most people are less irritable when they are well rested. Sometimes, if I'm not well rested even the littlest things can get on my nerves. It could be something as simple as someone speaking to me saying, hello how are you doing today? And I can cop an attitude. In November 2019, my beloved Grandfather passed away from old age. He was blessed to see 100 years on this earth. Nowadays, people can only dream about living to be 100 years old. Even though it's rare to see that age, there are still many others out there who do live to that great number and even higher. This particular death in my family was not an emotional one because my Grandfather lived a full life and was expected to die soon. So the night before the funeral, all of the family had come to attend his home going service. Including my sister. When we woke up the next morning to start getting ready for the funeral, I was extremely tired from work the night before. And it seemed like my sister had all the energy in the world! Oh, she was singing, dancing, and playing her music on her phone extremely loud. She was just in an amazing mood. And I wasn't faulting her for that. Meanwhile I'm sitting there looking like the Grinch Who Stole Christmas and Ebenezer Scrooge on steroids. She looked at me and said, what's wrong with you? I cut my eyes at her and said I'm tired tiffany! You know I had to work last night.

But you see, she was use to getting up early in the morning and I wasn't. After we got dressed, ate our breakfast, and made our way to the funeral I was fine. But it just took me a little while to get my head together because of how tired I was from working the night before. Please note, always make sure you are well rested before you set out on your day to tackle your endeavors. Also,

Breathing, prayer, and meditation may help with relaxation and sleep as well as some natural herbs and teas.

St. John's Wort

Popular in Europe, St. John's wort is an herbal treatment for depression. While American physicians do not fully endorse St. John's wort to the extent that some European doctors do, it may benefit individuals who do not have clinical depression but milder forms of depression. St. John's wort is also sold as a dietary supplement in the United States, where the standards for selling supplements are less strict than the standards for prescription or over-the-counter drugs. The supplement is most commonly used for "the blues", nervousness, tiredness, poor appetite, trouble sleeping, and anxiety. St. John's wort is also used for symptoms of menopause, and many other conditions, but there is no good scientific evidence to support these uses. (Please consult with your health care physician before considering taking St. John's wort).

Hot Kava

Kava root comes from the kava plant and has sedative attributes. It is a root used in relaxing teas. Some studies have revealed that kava is effective for relieving stress and anxiety, which may help alleviate depression symptoms. Kava is like chamomile on steroids. This muddy-tasting little root comes from the Pacific Islands, where people have used it for centuries as everything from a pain reliever to a ceremonial drink. A potent anxiety reliever, kava offers a non-alcoholic way to wind down at the end of the day, especially if you're working late or you have trouble sleeping. The secret lies in kavalactones, the psychoactive parts of the kava plant. The kavalatones in a cup of kava tea, or a few drops of kava extract, can put you into a rare state of relaxed focus. Just like St. John's Wort, Hot Kava is also a supplement that can be taken over the counter. (I also recommend that you consult with your healthcare physician before consumption)

Do Things You Used To Enjoy

When it comes to depression, it's all about your mood. Engaging in activities that once gave you joy may help you get back some of your positive energy and boost your mood again. Pick back up that hobby you used to love. Or change your routine altogether and get out of the house for a trip to a museum, the library, skating rink, a music event, or a volunteering event. These are all things that can contribute tremendously to your since of fulfillment and bring you back emotionally were you need to be.

Music

The right kind of music can help you relax, bring joy, and lift your mood as well. And do not just listen. Sometimes, music therapy involves singing along to your favorite tunes. Music has also been proven to decrease stress, so turn up the volume and dance a little dance! Take an outing to a concert, stream a live performance, or turn on the radio. Music is all around you, and it is a free path to treating your mood. I like to listen to a little bit of everything. R&B music, hip-hop, jazz music, heavy metal, and more. It really just all depends on what kind of mood that I'm in at that present time. But Lately, I've found myself loving to listen to plain old instrumentals. Not just any instrumentals. Beats that provide soothing effects for my mind, body, soul, and spirit. I'm a very laid back, chill, and light spirited kind of person. People tell me all the time that I'm very mature for my age. And that also goes along with the type of music that I love to listen to as well.

Jazzy and lofi hip-hop beats are two of my favorites. I mean, I can literally hit the open road, play some jazzy lofi music, and get lost all in the mix. If you ever get a chance, whether your in your car driving to your destination, at home relaxing, or even if you have a little free time at your job and you need something to help clear your mind. Check out lofi hip-hop or jazzy instrumentals beats on YouTube. I promise you, it will completely take you to another world.

Volunteer

Giving back through volunteering is a great way to get your mind off the things that bring you down. It also can foster a sense of accomplishment and give you energy by changing up your routine. And an added benefit is that you will be giving back to your community at the same time. A natural response to us not getting the things we want out of life is anger, sadness, and frustration. Sometimes, we can get so hell bent out of shape over the things we don't have, that we forget that it's always someone else out there who has it 10x worse than we do. If your helping a loved one out, or someone in your local community who needs a helping hand. It will bring you a sense of joy and happiness once the task is completed.

You can't be mad at your situation and pitiful about what's going on in your life, and joyful helping someone else out at the same time. It just won't work. Your brain won't allow you to. There have been so many situations in my life that I can't even start to list about a particular matter that I was so upset over. That once I transitioned and preoccupied my intentions to something else, I was able to reflect back over what had me upset. And I had no choice but to let it go. Volunteering and helping others out is an excellent way to get your mind off the obstacles you are facing.

Do Not Ignore Your Diet

When it comes to combating depression, anxiety, stress, and fear, what you eat is very important. While there is no diet that can cure depression (or the other disorders that are associated with it), there are certain vitamins and foods that can help regulate your mood and stimulate your mind.

For example, there are certain foods that contain hormones and preservatives that can affect your mood.

Hormones are frequently found in meats that are not grass-fed or organic. Other foods and beverages that can also affect your mood include caffeine, alcohol, and sugary foods that can make you crash. I really try to stick to a strict diet when it comes to my eating. Only having one cheat meal once a week. And the rest of my days, making sure that I'm filling up on plenty of high protein meats, vegetables, fruits, mixed nuts, and drinking plenty of water. I do a lot of vigorous and strenuous workouts. So I need to make sure that I'm putting the right amount of nutrients and substances back into my body to build lean muscle and a solid physique.

But here's the great part though. When it comes to my cheat day. I love to indulge in a slew of eating consisting of anything that I want for the entire day. It could be ice cream, pizza, cheeseburgers, cookies, honey buns, candy, fried chicken and more. Everything that your not supposed to eat gets consumed that day. My most prized and much appreciated dessert though is, made from scratch homemade oven cooked pecan pie. Talk about some good eating! One day, I was craving the taste of pecan pie so bad. I told my fiancé that we had to go to the Piggly Wiggly Grocery Store in Maysville NC immediately to pick up the ingredients to make one. Piggly Wiggly was the closest store to where we lived, plus we didn't feel like driving all the way back to New Bern in the opposite direction of us to go get it. Once we got it. On the way back home, the only thing that I could think about tasting that sweet, gooey, caramel like flavor. With that buttery textured piecrust. After preparing it, and letting it cook in the oven for about 40 to 45 minutes. Once I took it out. Within the first 10 to 15 minutes half of the pie was already gone! Being some what disgusted with myself for eating half of the pie so fast. I decided to jump into the shower to clean myself up. I then called my fiancé into the bathroom and said babe. You know the other half of that pie in there. She said yes. I said, throw the rest of it in the trash for me. She looked at me like I was crazy. She said, why? I said, because if you don't. I'm going to eat the whole entire thing! She busted out laughing and said ok honey whatever you say.

You know it's bad when it's to the point were you have to ask someone to throw the rest of your food away for you because you've eaten so much of it. But if I didn't ask her to do that for me, it would have gotten really out of hand. Normally, my cheat day runs every Saturday. And on Sundays, I make sure that I detox my entire body of what I ate from the previous day by drinking a bottle of Apple Cider Vinegar with the Mother. If you have never heard of this product, it has tons of benefits to help you cleanse your gastrointestinal tract out from all of it's impurities you are trying to get rid of.

Also, do not forget to take your vitamins on a regular daily basis. Vitamin B and folic acid deficiencies have been linked to depression. So be sure to take a good supplement or eat leafy greens, beans, eggs, and fruits high in folic acid and vitamin B.

Other supplements like Omega-3 fatty acids and Vitamin D can help stabilize your mood as well.

CONCLUSION

When it comes to mental illness as a whole, there is no need for a stigma. It is vitally important to eliminate the stigma that pervades mental illness in general, and in certain cultures. If the stigma remains, it can cause those who need treatment to avoid getting help. And that, in turn, can lead to severe mental health situations and issues.

Also, If you are in need you should be aware of and implement those low cost remedies noted in Chapter 6 to boost your mood including:

- Exercising
- Amending your schedule for small successes
- Relaxing
- Doing the things you once enjoyed and loved
- And maintaining a proper diet free of mood-altering hormones and preservatives

And always remember the number #1 key to overcoming anxiety, stress, and fear is to TAKE IT EASY ON YOURSELF! Life is already hard enough with unpredictable challenges, circumstances, and setbacks. Please do not assist the challenges of life and, what you are going through by beating yourself up mentally and emotionally as well.

Take care good friend.

Made in the USA
Columbia, SC
08 April 2021